From Munich to Pearl Harbor